This Planner Belongs to

_____

_____

Year: **Semester:**

Monday	Tuesday	Wednesday	Thursday	Friday	Saturday	Sunday

Notes:

Year: Semester:

Monday	Tuesday	Wednesday	Thursday	Friday	Saturday	Sunday

Notes:

Year: Semester:

Monday	Tuesday	Wednesday	Thursday	Friday	Saturday	Sunday

Notes:

Year: Semester:

Monday	Tuesday	Wednesday	Thursday	Friday	Saturday	Sunday

Notes:

Year: **Semester:**

Monday	Tuesday	Wednesday	Thursday	Friday	Saturday	Sunday

Notes:

Year: Semester:

Monday	Tuesday	Wednesday	Thursday	Friday	Saturday	Sunday

Notes:

Year: **Semester:**

Monday	Tuesday	Wednesday	Thursday	Friday	Saturday	Sunday

Notes:

Year: Semester:

Monday	Tuesday	Wednesday	Thursday	Friday	Saturday	Sunday

Notes:

Year: Semester:

Monday	Tuesday	Wednesday	Thursday	Friday	Saturday	Sunday

Notes:

Year: **Semester:**

Monday	Tuesday	Wednesday	Thursday	Friday	Saturday	Sunday

Notes:

Year: **Semester:**

Monday	Tuesday	Wednesday	Thursday	Friday	Saturday	Sunday

Notes:

Year: Semester:

Monday	Tuesday	Wednesday	Thursday	Friday	Saturday	Sunday

Notes:

Weekly Class Timetable

Date:

Time	Monday	Tuesday	Wednesday	Thursday	Friday
07 am					
08 am					
09 am					
10 am					
11 am					
12 pm					
01 pm					
02 pm					
03 pm					
04 pm					
05 pm					
06 pm					

Weekly Class Timetable

Date:

Time	Monday	Tuesday	Wednesday	Thursday	Friday
07 am					
08 am					
09 am					
10 am					
11 am					
12 pm					
01 pm					
02 pm					
03 pm					
04 pm					
05 pm					
06 pm					

Weekly Class Timetable

Date:

Time	Monday	Tuesday	Wednesday	Thursday	Friday
07 am					
08 am					
09 am					
10 am					
11 am					
12 pm					
01 pm					
02 pm					
03 pm					
04 pm					
05 pm					
06 pm					

Weekly Class Timetable

Date:

Time	Monday	Tuesday	Wednesday	Thursday	Friday
07 am					
08 am					
09 am					
10 am					
11 am					
12 pm					
01 pm					
02 pm					
03 pm					
04 pm					
05 pm					
06 pm					

Weekly Class Timetable

Date:

Time	Monday	Tuesday	Wednesday	Thursday	Friday
07 am					
08 am					
09 am					
10 am					
11 am					
12 pm					
01 pm					
02 pm					
03 pm					
04 pm					
05 pm					
06 pm					

Weekly Class Timetable

Date:

Time	Monday	Tuesday	Wednesday	Thursday	Friday
07 am					
08 am					
09 am					
10 am					
11 am					
12 pm					
01 pm					
02 pm					
03 pm					
04 pm					
05 pm					
06 pm					

Weekly Class Timetable

Date:

Time	Monday	Tuesday	Wednesday	Thursday	Friday
07 am					
08 am					
09 am					
10 am					
11 am					
12 pm					
01 pm					
02 pm					
03 pm					
04 pm					
05 pm					
06 pm					

Weekly Class Timetable

Date:

Time	Monday	Tuesday	Wednesday	Thursday	Friday
07 am					
08 am					
09 am					
10 am					
11 am					
12 pm					
01 pm					
02 pm					
03 pm					
04 pm					
05 pm					
06 pm					

Weekly Class Timetable

Date:

Time	Monday	Tuesday	Wednesday	Thursday	Friday
07 am					
08 am					
09 am					
10 am					
11 am					
12 pm					
01 pm					
02 pm					
03 pm					
04 pm					
05 pm					
06 pm					

Weekly Class Timetable

Date:

Time	Monday	Tuesday	Wednesday	Thursday	Friday
07 am					
08 am					
09 am					
10 am					
11 am					
12 pm					
01 pm					
02 pm					
03 pm					
04 pm					
05 pm					
06 pm					

Weekly Class Timetable

Date:

Time	Monday	Tuesday	Wednesday	Thursday	Friday
07 am					
08 am					
09 am					
10 am					
11 am					
12 pm					
01 pm					
02 pm					
03 pm					
04 pm					
05 pm					
06 pm					

Weekly Class Timetable

Date:

Time	Monday	Tuesday	Wednesday	Thursday	Friday
07 am					
08 am					
09 am					
10 am					
11 am					
12 pm					
01 pm					
02 pm					
03 pm					
04 pm					
05 pm					
06 pm					

Weekly Planner

Goals

_____
_____
_____
_____
_____

To do list

_____
_____
_____
_____
_____
_____
_____
_____

Date:

Monday	
Tuesday	
Wednesday	
Thursday	
Friday	
Saturday	
Sunday	

To study

_____
_____
_____
_____
_____
_____
_____

Important events

_____
_____
_____
_____
_____
_____

Notes

_____
_____

Weekly Planner

Goals

_____
_____
_____
_____
_____

To do list

_____
_____
_____
_____
_____
_____
_____
_____

Date:

Monday	
Tuesday	
Wednesday	
Thursday	
Friday	
Saturday	
Sunday	

To study

_____
_____
_____
_____
_____
_____
_____

Important events

_____
_____
_____
_____
_____
_____

Notes

_____
_____
_____

Weekly Planner

Goals

To do list

Date:

Monday	
Tuesday	
Wednesday	
Thursday	
Friday	
Saturday	
Sunday	

To study

Important events

Notes

Weekly Planner

Goals

To do list

Date:

Monday	
Tuesday	
Wednesday	
Thursday	
Friday	
Saturday	
Sunday	

To study

Important events

Notes

Weekly Planner

Goals

To do list

Date:

Monday	
Tuesday	
Wednesday	
Thursday	
Friday	
Saturday	
Sunday	

To study

Important events

Notes

Weekly Planner

Goals

_____
_____
_____
_____
_____

Date:

Monday	
Tuesday	
Wednesday	
Thursday	
Friday	
Saturday	
Sunday	

To do list

_____
_____
_____
_____
_____
_____
_____
_____

To study

_____
_____
_____
_____
_____
_____

Important events

_____
_____
_____
_____
_____
_____

Notes

_____
_____

Weekly Planner

Goals

_____
_____
_____
_____
_____

Date:

Monday	
Tuesday	
Wednesday	
Thursday	
Friday	
Saturday	
Sunday	

To do list

_____
_____
_____
_____
_____
_____
_____
_____

To study

_____
_____
_____
_____
_____
_____

Important events

_____
_____
_____
_____
_____
_____

Notes

_____

Weekly Planner

Goals

To do list

Date:

Monday	
Tuesday	
Wednesday	
Thursday	
Friday	
Saturday	
Sunday	

To study

Important events

Notes

Weekly Planner

Goals

_____
_____
_____
_____
_____

To do list

_____
_____
_____
_____
_____
_____
_____
_____

Date:

Monday	
Tuesday	
Wednesday	
Thursday	
Friday	
Saturday	
Sunday	

To study

_____
_____
_____
_____
_____

Important events

_____
_____
_____
_____
_____
_____

Notes

_____

Weekly Planner

Goals

_____
_____
_____
_____
_____
_____

To do list

_____
_____
_____
_____
_____
_____
_____
_____

Date:

Monday	
Tuesday	
Wednesday	
Thursday	
Friday	
Saturday	
Sunday	

To study

_____
_____
_____
_____
_____
_____
_____
_____

Important events

_____
_____
_____
_____
_____
_____
_____

Notes

_____
_____

Weekly Planner

Goals
_____
_____
_____
_____
_____

To do list
_____
_____
_____
_____
_____
_____
_____
_____

Date:

Monday	
Tuesday	
Wednesday	
Thursday	
Friday	
Saturday	
Sunday	

To study
_____
_____
_____
_____
_____
_____
_____

Important events
_____
_____
_____
_____
_____
_____

Notes
_____
_____

Weekly Planner

Goals

_____
_____
_____
_____
_____

To do list

_____
_____
_____
_____
_____
_____
_____
_____

Date:

Monday	
Tuesday	
Wednesday	
Thursday	
Friday	
Saturday	
Sunday	

To study

_____
_____
_____
_____
_____
_____

Important events

_____
_____
_____
_____
_____
_____

Notes

_____
_____

Weekly Planner

Goals

To do list

Date:

Monday	
Tuesday	
Wednesday	
Thursday	
Friday	
Saturday	
Sunday	

To study

Important events

Notes

Weekly Planner

Goals

To do list

Date:

Monday	
Tuesday	
Wednesday	
Thursday	
Friday	
Saturday	
Sunday	

To study

Important events

Notes

Weekly Planner

Goals
_____
_____
_____
_____
_____

Date:

Monday	
Tuesday	
Wednesday	
Thursday	
Friday	
Saturday	
Sunday	

To do list
_____
_____
_____
_____
_____
_____
_____
_____
_____

To study
_____
_____
_____
_____
_____
_____

Important events
_____
_____
_____
_____
_____

Notes
_____
_____

Weekly Planner

Goals

_____
_____
_____
_____
_____

To do list

_____
_____
_____
_____
_____
_____
_____
_____

Date:

Monday	
Tuesday	
Wednesday	
Thursday	
Friday	
Saturday	
Sunday	

To study

_____
_____
_____
_____
_____
_____
_____

Important events

_____
_____
_____
_____
_____
_____

Notes

_____
_____

Weekly Planner

Goals

To do list

Date:

Monday	
Tuesday	
Wednesday	
Thursday	
Friday	
Saturday	
Sunday	

To study

Important events

Notes

Weekly Planner

Goals

To do list

Date:

Monday	
Tuesday	
Wednesday	
Thursday	
Friday	
Saturday	
Sunday	

To study

Important events

Notes

Weekly Planner

Goals

_____
_____
_____
_____
_____

Date:

Monday	
Tuesday	
Wednesday	
Thursday	
Friday	
Saturday	
Sunday	

To do list

_____
_____
_____
_____
_____
_____
_____
_____
_____

To study

_____
_____
_____
_____
_____
_____

Important events

_____
_____
_____
_____
_____
_____

Notes

_____
_____

Weekly Planner

Goals

_____
_____
_____
_____
_____

To do list

_____
_____
_____
_____
_____
_____
_____
_____

Date:

Monday	
Tuesday	
Wednesday	
Thursday	
Friday	
Saturday	
Sunday	

To study

_____
_____
_____
_____
_____
_____

Important events

_____
_____
_____
_____
_____

Notes

_____
_____

Weekly Planner

Goals

_____
_____
_____
_____

To do list

_____
_____
_____
_____
_____
_____
_____

Date:

Monday	
Tuesday	
Wednesday	
Thursday	
Friday	
Saturday	
Sunday	

To study

_____
_____
_____
_____
_____

Important events

_____
_____
_____
_____
_____

Notes

_____
_____

Weekly Planner

Goals

_____
_____
_____
_____
_____

Date:

Monday	
Tuesday	
Wednesday	
Thursday	
Friday	
Saturday	
Sunday	

To do list

_____
_____
_____
_____
_____
_____
_____

To study

_____
_____
_____
_____
_____
_____
_____

Important events

_____
_____
_____
_____
_____

Notes

_____
_____

Weekly Planner

Goals

_____
_____
_____
_____
_____

To do list

_____
_____
_____
_____
_____
_____
_____
_____

Date:

Monday	
Tuesday	
Wednesday	
Thursday	
Friday	
Saturday	
Sunday	

To study

_____
_____
_____
_____
_____
_____

Important events

_____
_____
_____
_____
_____

Notes

_____
_____

Weekly Planner

Goals
_____
_____
_____
_____
_____

To do list
_____
_____
_____
_____
_____

Date:

Monday	
Tuesday	
Wednesday	
Thursday	
Friday	
Saturday	
Sunday	

To study
_____
_____
_____
_____
_____

Important events
_____
_____
_____
_____

Notes
_____
_____

Weekly Planner

Goals

_____
_____
_____
_____
_____

Date:

Monday	
Tuesday	
Wednesday	
Thursday	
Friday	
Saturday	
Sunday	

To do list

_____
_____
_____
_____
_____
_____
_____

To study

_____
_____
_____
_____
_____
_____

Important events

_____
_____
_____
_____
_____

Notes

_____

Weekly Planner

Goals
_____
_____
_____
_____
_____

To do list
_____
_____
_____
_____
_____
_____
_____

Date:

Monday	
Tuesday	
Wednesday	
Thursday	
Friday	
Saturday	
Sunday	

To study
_____
_____
_____
_____
_____
_____

Important events
_____
_____
_____
_____
_____
_____

Notes
_____
_____

Weekly Planner

Goals _____

_____
_____
_____
_____

To do list _____

_____
_____
_____
_____
_____
_____
_____

Date:

Monday	
Tuesday	
Wednesday	
Thursday	
Friday	
Saturday	
Sunday	

To study _____

_____
_____
_____
_____
_____
_____

Important events _____

_____
_____
_____
_____
_____

Notes _____

_____

Weekly Planner

Goals

_____
_____
_____
_____
_____

To do list

_____
_____
_____
_____
_____
_____
_____
_____

Date:

Monday	
Tuesday	
Wednesday	
Thursday	
Friday	
Saturday	
Sunday	

To study

_____
_____
_____
_____
_____
_____

Important events

_____
_____
_____
_____
_____

Notes

_____
_____

Weekly Planner

Goals
_____
_____
_____
_____
_____

Date:

Monday	
Tuesday	
Wednesday	
Thursday	
Friday	
Saturday	
Sunday	

To do list
_____
_____
_____
_____
_____
_____
_____
_____

To study
_____
_____
_____
_____
_____
_____
_____

Important events
_____
_____
_____
_____
_____
_____

Notes
_____
_____

Weekly Planner

Goals

_____
_____
_____
_____
_____

Date:

Monday	
Tuesday	
Wednesday	
Thursday	
Friday	
Saturday	
Sunday	

To do list

_____
_____
_____
_____
_____
_____
_____

To study

_____
_____
_____
_____
_____
_____
_____

Important events

_____
_____
_____
_____
_____
_____

Notes

_____
_____

Study Planner

Date:

Subject to study

_____
_____
_____
_____

Chapters for today

_____
_____
_____
_____

Hours to study
Planned:
Actual:

Most important:

Time		Time	
04 am		02 pm	
05 am		03 pm	
06 am		04 pm	
07 am		05 pm	
8 am		06 pm	
09 am		07 pm	
10 am		08 pm	
11 am		09 pm	
12 pm		10 pm	
01 pm		11 pm	

Study Planner

Date:

Subject to study

_____
_____
_____
_____

Chapters for today

_____
_____
_____
_____

Hours to study
Planned:
Actual:

Most important:

Time		Time	
04 am		02 pm	
05 am		03 pm	
06 am		04 pm	
07 am		05 pm	
8 am		06 pm	
09 am		07 pm	
10 am		08 pm	
11 am		09 pm	
12 pm		10 pm	
01 pm		11 pm	

Study Planner

Date:

Subject to study

_____
_____
_____
_____

Chapters for today

_____
_____
_____
_____

Hours to study
Planned:
Actual:

Most important:

Time		Time	
04 am		02 pm	
05 am		03 pm	
06 am		04 pm	
07 am		05 pm	
8 am		06 pm	
09 am		07 pm	
10 am		08 pm	
11 am		09 pm	
12 pm		10 pm	
01 pm		11 pm	

Study Planner

Date:

Subject to study

Chapters for today

Hours to study
Planned:
Actual:

Most important:

Time		Time	
04 am		02 pm	
05 am		03 pm	
06 am		04 pm	
07 am		05 pm	
8 am		06 pm	
09 am		07 pm	
10 am		08 pm	
11 am		09 pm	
12 pm		10 pm	
01 pm		11 pm	

Study Planner

Date:

Subject to study

_____
_____
_____
_____

Chapters for today

_____
_____
_____
_____

Hours to study
Planned:
Actual:

Most important:

Time		Time	
04 am		02 pm	
05 am		03 pm	
06 am		04 pm	
07 am		05 pm	
8 am		06 pm	
09 am		07 pm	
10 am		08 pm	
11 am		09 pm	
12 pm		10 pm	
01 pm		11 pm	

Study Planner

Date:

Subject to study

_____
_____
_____
_____
_____

Chapters for today

_____
_____
_____
_____
_____

Hours to study
Planned:
Actual:

Most important:

Time		Time	
04 am		02 pm	
05 am		03 pm	
06 am		04 pm	
07 am		05 pm	
8 am		06 pm	
09 am		07 pm	
10 am		08 pm	
11 am		09 pm	
12 pm		10 pm	
01 pm		11 pm	

Study Planner

Date:

Subject to study

_____
_____
_____
_____

Chapters for today

_____
_____
_____
_____

Hours to study
Planned:
Actual:

Most important:

Time		Time	
04 am		02 pm	
05 am		03 pm	
06 am		04 pm	
07 am		05 pm	
8 am		06 pm	
09 am		07 pm	
10 am		08 pm	
11 am		09 pm	
12 pm		10 pm	
01 pm		11 pm	

Study Planner

Date:

Subject to study

_____
_____
_____
_____

Chapters for today

_____
_____
_____
_____

Hours to study
Planned:
Actual:

Most important:

Time		Time	
04 am		02 pm	
05 am		03 pm	
06 am		04 pm	
07 am		05 pm	
8 am		06 pm	
09 am		07 pm	
10 am		08 pm	
11 am		09 pm	
12 pm		10 pm	
01 pm		11 pm	

Study Planner

Date:

Subject to study
_____
_____
_____
_____

Chapters for today
_____
_____
_____
_____

Hours to study
Planned:
Actual:

Most important:

Time		Time	
04 am		02 pm	
05 am		03 pm	
06 am		04 pm	
07 am		05 pm	
8 am		06 pm	
09 am		07 pm	
10 am		08 pm	
11 am		09 pm	
12 pm		10 pm	
01 pm		11 pm	

Study Planner

Date:

Subject to study

_____
_____
_____
_____
_____

Chapters for today

_____
_____
_____
_____
_____

Hours to study
Planned:
Actual:

Most important:

Time		Time	
04 am		02 pm	
05 am		03 pm	
06 am		04 pm	
07 am		05 pm	
8 am		06 pm	
09 am		07 pm	
10 am		08 pm	
11 am		09 pm	
12 pm		10 pm	
01 pm		11 pm	

Study Planner

Date:

Subject to study

_____
_____
_____
_____
_____

Chapters for today

_____
_____
_____
_____
_____

Hours to study
Planned:
Actual:

Most important:

Time		Time	
04 am		02 pm	
05 am		03 pm	
06 am		04 pm	
07 am		05 pm	
8 am		06 pm	
09 am		07 pm	
10 am		08 pm	
11 am		09 pm	
12 pm		10 pm	
01 pm		11 pm	

Study Planner

Date:

Subject to study
_____
_____
_____
_____

Chapters for today
_____
_____
_____
_____

Hours to study
Planned:
Actual:

Most important:

Time		Time	
04 am		02 pm	
05 am		03 pm	
06 am		04 pm	
07 am		05 pm	
8 am		06 pm	
09 am		07 pm	
10 am		08 pm	
11 am		09 pm	
12 pm		10 pm	
01 pm		11 pm	

Study Planner

Date:

Subject to study

_____
_____
_____
_____

Chapters for today

_____
_____
_____
_____

Hours to study
Planned:
Actual:

Most important:

Time		Time	
04 am		02 pm	
05 am		03 pm	
06 am		04 pm	
07 am		05 pm	
8 am		06 pm	
09 am		07 pm	
10 am		08 pm	
11 am		09 pm	
12 pm		10 pm	
01 pm		11 pm	

Study Planner

Date:

Subject to study

_____
_____
_____
_____
_____

Chapters for today

_____
_____
_____
_____
_____

Hours to study
Planned:
Actual:

Most important:

Time		Time	
04 am		02 pm	
05 am		03 pm	
06 am		04 pm	
07 am		05 pm	
8 am		06 pm	
09 am		07 pm	
10 am		08 pm	
11 am		09 pm	
12 pm		10 pm	
01 pm		11 pm	

Study Planner

Date:

Subject to study

Chapters for today

Hours to study
Planned:
Actual:

Most important:

Time		Time	
04 am		02 pm	
05 am		03 pm	
06 am		04 pm	
07 am		05 pm	
8 am		06 pm	
09 am		07 pm	
10 am		08 pm	
11 am		09 pm	
12 pm		10 pm	
01 pm		11 pm	

Study Planner

Date:

Subject to study

_____
_____
_____
_____

Chapters for today

_____
_____
_____
_____

Hours to study
Planned:
Actual:

Most important:

Time		Time	
04 am		02 pm	
05 am		03 pm	
06 am		04 pm	
07 am		05 pm	
8 am		06 pm	
09 am		07 pm	
10 am		08 pm	
11 am		09 pm	
12 pm		10 pm	
01 pm		11 pm	

Study Planner

Date:

Subject to study

_____
_____
_____
_____

Chapters for today

_____
_____
_____
_____

Hours to study
Planned:
Actual:

Most important:

Time		Time	
04 am		02 pm	
05 am		03 pm	
06 am		04 pm	
07 am		05 pm	
8 am		06 pm	
09 am		07 pm	
10 am		08 pm	
11 am		09 pm	
12 pm		10 pm	
01 pm		11 pm	

Study Planner

Date:

Subject to study

Chapters for today

Hours to study
Planned:
Actual:

Most important:

Time		Time	
04 am		02 pm	
05 am		03 pm	
06 am		04 pm	
07 am		05 pm	
8 am		06 pm	
09 am		07 pm	
10 am		08 pm	
11 am		09 pm	
12 pm		10 pm	
01 pm		11 pm	

Study Planner

Date:

Subject to study
_____
_____
_____
_____

Chapters for today
_____
_____
_____
_____

Hours to study
Planned:
Actual:

Most important:

Time		Time	
04 am		02 pm	
05 am		03 pm	
06 am		04 pm	
07 am		05 pm	
8 am		06 pm	
09 am		07 pm	
10 am		08 pm	
11 am		09 pm	
12 pm		10 pm	
01 pm		11 pm	

Study Planner

Date:

Subject to study

Chapters for today

Hours to study
Planned:
Actual:

Most important:

Time		Time	
04 am		02 pm	
05 am		03 pm	
06 am		04 pm	
07 am		05 pm	
8 am		06 pm	
09 am		07 pm	
10 am		08 pm	
11 am		09 pm	
12 pm		10 pm	
01 pm		11 pm	

Study Planner

Date:

Subject to study

_____
_____
_____
_____

Chapters for today

_____
_____
_____
_____

Hours to study
Planned:
Actual:

Most important:

Time		Time	
04 am		02 pm	
05 am		03 pm	
06 am		04 pm	
07 am		05 pm	
8 am		06 pm	
09 am		07 pm	
10 am		08 pm	
11 am		09 pm	
12 pm		10 pm	
01 pm		11 pm	

Study Planner

Date:

Subject to study

Chapters for today

Hours to study
Planned:
Actual:

Most important:

Time		Time	
04 am		02 pm	
05 am		03 pm	
06 am		04 pm	
07 am		05 pm	
8 am		06 pm	
09 am		07 pm	
10 am		08 pm	
11 am		09 pm	
12 pm		10 pm	
01 pm		11 pm	

Study Planner

Date:

Subject to study

Chapters for today

Hours to study
Planned:
Actual:

Most important:

Time		Time	
04 am		02 pm	
05 am		03 pm	
06 am		04 pm	
07 am		05 pm	
8 am		06 pm	
09 am		07 pm	
10 am		08 pm	
11 am		09 pm	
12 pm		10 pm	
01 pm		11 pm	

Study Planner

Date:

Subject to study

Chapters for today

Hours to study
Planned:
Actual:

Most important:

Time		Time	
04 am		02 pm	
05 am		03 pm	
06 am		04 pm	
07 am		05 pm	
8 am		06 pm	
09 am		07 pm	
10 am		08 pm	
11 am		09 pm	
12 pm		10 pm	
01 pm		11 pm	

Study Planner

Date: _____

Subject to study
_____
_____
_____
_____

Chapters for today
_____
_____
_____
_____

Hours to study
Planned:
Actual:

Most important:

Time		Time	
04 am		02 pm	
05 am		03 pm	
06 am		04 pm	
07 am		05 pm	
8 am		06 pm	
09 am		07 pm	
10 am		08 pm	
11 am		09 pm	
12 pm		10 pm	
01 pm		11 pm	

Study Planner

Date:

Subject to study

_____
_____
_____
_____

Chapters for today

_____
_____
_____
_____

Hours to study
Planned:
Actual:

Most important:

Time		Time	
04 am		02 pm	
05 am		03 pm	
06 am		04 pm	
07 am		05 pm	
8 am		06 pm	
09 am		07 pm	
10 am		08 pm	
11 am		09 pm	
12 pm		10 pm	
01 pm		11 pm	

Assignment tracker

Subject: **Date:**

Assignment	Due date	Score

Assignment tracker

Subject: **Date:**

Assignment	Due date	Score

Assignment tracker

Subject: **Date:**

Assignment	Due date	Score

Assignment tracker

Subject: **Date:**

Assignment	Due date	Score

Assignment tracker

Subject: **Date:**

Assignment	Due date	Score

Assignment tracker

Subject: **Date:**

Assignment	Due date	Score

Assignment tracker

Subject: Date:

Assignment	Due date	Score

Assignment tracker

Subject: **Date:**

Assignment	Due date	Score

Assignment tracker

Subject: **Date:**

Assignment	Due date	Score

Assignment tracker

Subject: Date:

Assignment	Due date	Score

Assignment tracker

Subject: Date:

Assignment	Due date	Score

Assignment tracker

Subject: **Date:**

Assignment	Due date	Score

Assignment tracker

Subject: **Date:**

Assignment	Due date	Score

Assignment tracker

Subject: **Date:**

Assignment	Due date	Score

Assignment tracker

Subject: **Date:**

Assignment	Due date	Score

Assignment tracker

Subject: **Date:**

Assignment	Due date	Score

Assignment tracker

Subject: **Date:**

Assignment	Due date	Score

Assignment tracker

Subject: **Date:**

Assignment	Due date	Score

Grade tracker

Subject:

Date	Topic	Score	Passed

Grade tracker

Subject:

Date	Topic	Score	Passed

Grade tracker

Subject:

Date	Topic	Score	Passed

Grade tracker

Subject:

Date	Topic	Score	Passed

Grade tracker

Subject:

Date	Topic	Score	Passed

Grade tracker

Subject:

Date	Topic	Score	Passed

Grade tracker

Subject:

Date	Topic	Score	Passed

Grade tracker

Subject:

Date	Topic	Score	Passed

Grade tracker

Subject:

Date	Topic	Score	Passed

Grade tracker

Subject:

Date	Topic	Score	Passed

Grade tracker

Subject:

Date	Topic	Score	Passed

Grade tracker

Subject:

Date	Topic	Score	Passed

www.ingramcontent.com/pod-product-compliance
Lightning Source LLC
LaVergne TN
LVHW060203080526
838202LV00052B/4191